To: Thomas Counts

Thank You For You

Support!

# One Step at a Time

*Growing up in Compton, California in the 1990's wasn't easy for anyone, especially a child with a deceased mother and a part-time father. Young Joseph Rivers was left in the care of his loving grandmother who took him in and raised him as her own—implanting educational morals in his life. As Rivers grew up he became determined to take a stand, linking the importance of education in fulfilling one's dreams through adversities. However, never-ending conflicts from family, friends, school bullies, local gang members, and strangers threatened Rivers' plan to succeed as well as dreams that were trying to be achieved. But with each obstacle came new challenges allowing lessons to be learned, including the ability to cope and most of all discover the true meaning of success.*

# A YOUNG MAN WITH A PLAN

A MEMOIR BY
Joseph Anthony Rivers

EDITED BY GARY BRIN

USA PUBLICATIONS
a division of Book Company Publishing, LLC

An original release of USA Publications, a division of
Book Company Publishing, LLC

All photographs are from the personal collection of Joseph Anthony
Rivers. Images have been digitally enhanced for this edition.

Cover image by Dawson Design of Los Angeles.

ISBN—978-0-9830508-1-0

MANUFACTURED IN THE UNITED STATES OF AMERICA

This story is dedicated to my mother Kim Shallowhorn whom I know is smiling down from the heavens up above. I love you with all my heart and know you are proud of the man I have become.

# Contents

Acknowledgements ................................................. 11

Foreword ............................................................... 17

Preface ................................................................. 19

Introduction ........................................................ 23

1-Born into Misery.............................................. 27

2-Incapable Father .............................................. 36

3-Raids ................................................................ 44

4-My Plan Starts Now ......................................... 51

5-Bad News.......................................................... 56

6-Alone, but Saved by a Teacher .......................... 63

7-Perseverance, Faith, & Honesty ........................ 71

8-Life with an Unknown Father............................ 79

9-Issues, Lessons, & Family Problems................... 85

10-First Day......................................................... 92

11-Peer Pressure ................................................. 99

12-The End of the Beginning .............................. 106

About the Author & Editor................................. 108

# Acknowledgements

This has truly been an amazing journey. I have had the opportunity to meet many new wonderful people along the way who not only encouraged me at times but motivated me to be better. Life is not always about taking but sometimes about what you can give and how you can impact the lives of others through your experiences. This is a very important section for me because it gives me the chance to thank everyone individually for the way they have impacted my life whether it was from a financial aspect all the way down to the kind and thoughtful words of encouragement or advice.

I would first like to thank God. He has been my guide through this entire project. There were many times I thought I would give up or quit but with his assurance I knew that I was destined to persevere through my adversities. Writing this book wasn't as nearly as hard as I thought it would be because I could feel God's hand guiding me. I thank you for all that you have blessed me with and the talent that you have given me to motivate and inspire others to be all they can be through my writings of past experiences.

To my loving mother Kim Shallowhorn, you are my heart and I live to see you smile down upon me. I know you are in the heavens up above cheering graciously as I strive for greatness. You will always be my motivation, my spark, and my will to succeed. For years, I questioned why my mother? Why did God have to take my mom? But now as I look up I know you're in a better place and we will meet again soon. Writing this portion of my acknowledgements to you has brought me tears of joy. I love you so much and pray that you are proud of me. I can't wait until the day that we can once again be together. I LOVE YOU with all my heart and may you REST IN PEACE my dear mother.

Next, I would like to thank someone who has been there for me since day one, my grandmother, Edna Shallowhorn. Words cannot truly express how grateful and appreciative I am to have you in my life. You have encouraged me to reach for the stars while valuing education. The little things you have done in my life are now so much clearer when I look back. It takes me back to the days when you would not let me go outside until I did my homework. I didn't understand what was so important about doing my homework at that moment or later but now as young man I can see that you were implanting education morals to become my first priority. I thank you for everything you have done for me. I thank God for placing you in my life and I love with all my heart.

When thinking about acknowledgments one of the first names that came to my mind was Gary Brin. Not many would understand the gratitude that I have for Gary other than him being my publisher, agent, editor, etc. He has been all of the above and more, not just for this project but in my life personally. When I needed advice he was there to help guide me in the right direction. When I didn't know about a particular subject he was there to educate me. I believe in fate and know that Gary and I working together on this project were meant to be. When I answered his Craigslist ad looking for talented writers I never thought he would actually fall in love with my material as I had. We share a common bond. This common bond proves that anything can be accomplished with hard work and dedication. I thank Gary for giving me the chance to show the world what I have to offer and most of all aiding me in accomplishing my dreams. You will always be a sacred part of my life and may God continue to bless you.

Cris Dawson I would like to thank you for your wonderful graphic design and commitment to *A Young Man with a Plan*. I thank you for all you have done and pray that God continues to bless you. You are truly a wonderful person.

Forgiveness is something I acquired over the years. I never really knew what was going on with our relationship or why we could never be the perfect father and son. However, I thank you Joseph Rivers. Although, we rarely see eye to eye I learned so much from you and I appreciate you dearly. You taught me the right from wrong as well as how important it is to be in my children's life one day. This book was not created to attack you in any way but rather allowed me to tell my story exactly the way it had happened. I recently learned at the age of 19 from my Aunt Thea that parents are not given handbooks on how to be parents and neither are they trained on the right and wrong ways of parenthood. I FORGIVE YOU and hold no grudges and hope one day we can rekindle our father-son relationship. I love you and may God bless you.

I recently learned also from a professor that every individual that contributes to a project even on a minimal level should be thanked because without them you wouldn't be where you are today. I would first like to thank my Aunt Thea Shallowhorn. You are truly a blessing and I thank you for what you have done in my life. You have been another mother figure and I truly appreciate you. With each story you have shared with me about my mother they have been key points in my development and I am sincerely grateful. May God continue to bless you in all your future endeavors. To my Aunt Freda Shallowhorn thanks for the motivation you have implanted within me to "Dream Big." You have always supported me in everything I have done. I greatly appreciate you and know that because of you I am a more determined and motivated individual today, may God continue to bless you. To my sister Starnisha Rivers, I love you with all my heart and know that our mother is smiling down from the heavens, applauding the strong, independent young woman you have become today. To my brothers, Amir and D'Jon I love you and may you continue to succeed and capture God's wonderful blessings he has in store for you guys. To my cousin Britney Jackson, I thank you for all you have done not just for me but for the *A Young Man with a Plan* project. You contributed to this project with your heart in which you gave numerous donations to the project. I love you and I'm so proud of the woman you have become today, may God bless you. To my favorite three younger cousins Raymond Tribble, Halle Pope, and Antowaniece Parker, I'm glad that I was able to inspire you guys educationally. You guys may have thought I was being competitive when I made comparisons between our report cards or thought I wanted to make you guys look bad. But I wanted you guys to surpass what I had done. I want you guys to be better than me. I'm so proud of all your academic achievements and love you guys with all my heart, may God continue to bless you. If I continued to thank everyone in depth my acknowledgments would be another book in itself so these names are those who I thank and love from the bottom of my heart. Joy Bautista, Cheryl Milburn, Symone Martin, Wanda Rivers, Darrell Pope, John Pope, Andi Walker, Ronald Tribble Sr., Diane Tribble, Ronald Tribble Jr., Ronnie Tribble III (Ronnie), Antoine Jackson, Anthony Jackson, Joseph Seale, Corey Muhammad, Shaheed Muhammad, Carla Lipscomb, Dorothy Bennet, Barbara Dorsey, Shirley Lee Dorsey, Charles Dorsey, James Dorsey, Rose Marie Love, Dorothy Brown, Clara Taylor, Bobby Dorsey, Rochelle Jackson, Roosevelt Young, Betty Dorsey, Sherri Price, Mary Naves, Albert Wiley, Reggie Calbert, Steven Reeves, JaQuan Kelly, Ardana Bonds, Deandre Thomas, Tracy Smith, Wanda Cross, Dominique Cross, Damien Bonds, Kevina McKinney, and for those of you I forgot I am truly sorry but know I love you all from the bottom of my heart. May God continue to bless you all.

I would also like to thank these individuals who contributed financially to the book. Edna Shallowhorn,

Dorothy Bennett, Britney Jackson, Larry Buford, Clara Taylor, Toni Brown, Elder Michael Cummings, John Legend, Steve Harvey, The Gates Millennium Scholars, & James Dorsey.

Joseph Anthony Rivers
November, 2010

# Foreword

This book came to my attention via an ad I placed on Craigslist looking for new writers of which to publish. There were many responses but few were willing to go that extra mile that Joseph Rivers was willing to go in order to guarantee their work was published. A writer that expects others to do their job for them after they turn in a manuscript can expect zero success. A writer needs to understand that writing a book is just the beginning. Endless revisions, lots of criticism, and editorial input must be expected in order to see one's book become a published reality. I knew this book was something special when I first started skimming it after Joseph emailed me the rough draft, but after fully reading it, not only do you understand what it feels to be a part of his life, you realize you know or knew people just like those he describes. It doesn't matter if you live in a big city or a small town, people are people. Dysfunctional families are unfortunately everywhere. It would be great if life played out on the set of a TV show, with every type of problem being solved after the last commercial break, but it just isn't so. Real life comes with many problems that cannot be solved right away, if ever. But lessons can be learned from every situation someone faces. What we do with these lessons are up to us. Blaming others for your faults is not the way—it only leads to further dysfunction in families and society.

The message in this book is simple, before you blame someone else for your mistakes, take a good look in the mirror and see what you can do to make your life better. Chances are you will find the answers you seek staring right back at you.

This book was edited from the original copy. However, in order to preserve the voice of the writer, certain word usage has been retained and while it may seem to be a publishing error to someone unfamiliar with this type of English dialect—it was intentional.

Gary Brin
Honolulu, 2010

## Preface

Decisions play important factors in shaping us as individuals into who we are today. There are some decisions that can change one's life, altering his or her future for better or worse. However, it is entirely up to the individual to either excel to new heights in life or let the obstacles that lie in the path of success distract them from the plan that has been instilled in us, not some of us, but all of us; often known as our destiny.

Who's to say that the obstacles that we experience as people constrain the success of our future? Many young adults today, believe being raised in tough environments, living in gang-ridden streets, growing up with no father, etc. is to blame, not only for their characteristic traits, but for their deprived successes. We see disarrayed young adults everyday in our streets who we categorize by the actions they display. The majority of the population would consider a young adult whose pants are sagging below his waist, showing his underwear, has multiple tattoos, and an abrupt slang as someone who is involved with malicious activity in their neighborhood, but that is not always true.

I grew up in the streets of Compton, California.

Compton is a city known to violence, drugs, crime, and even death. The 90's is known as the murder movement to many in Compton. This is said because the murder rate for Compton in the 90's was one of the highest of any other city. The city was split into various gang units, with the two most common groups, the Bloods and Crips, leading the way.

Compton was not the city you see on TV of a beautiful utopian city with citizens walking peacefully and embracing each other, not as strangers, but as friends. In fact, seeing high-positioned employed individuals was very rare. There were no lawyers, businessmen, or doctors in the part of Compton where I was from, but you did see the typical everyday drug dealer on the corner selling cocaine, or a junkie feigning for the drugs, trying to hustle money by begging the hardworking citizens who were providing for their families.

Losing my mother to an aneurism only made my life much more difficult to bear. I was brought into a world not having the luxury of having my mother attend my accomplished events or watch me grow into the man I am today. However, I had loving family members who cared about my well-being, although, at times, needless aggressive conflicts almost destroyed the family-oriented bond that we shared. The events in my life taught me to cope with my environment; learning its surroundings and, mostly, set myself apart from other individuals.

Although the city of Compton was a tough reality for me to reside in, it taught me many lifelong lessons that were needed for my mind to blossom in order to know the courage and integrity I possessed. The special gift that God had given me was the ability to reflect and learn from experiences which I applied to each potential obstacle that stood in my way. With so much intelligence at hand, I grasped on to what I call my three-part perseverance system, which consists of my goal, aspiration, and dream.

Inspired to help others due to the family incidences I had witnessed over the years, I decided to make a promise to myself in which I vowed, "No matter what stands in my way, I will accomplish my dreams." Being introduced to so much negativity almost shattered this promise countless times, but with faith and hope, I knew anything is possible.

This story is not to persuade you to believe as I do, but give you testimony to some of the same events or tragedies that you've probably experienced or are experiencing. Sometimes, we come to a certain point in time when we do not know how to handle certain situations or feel we are alone. Sometimes we can be pressured into doing things that make us feel uncomfortable just to fit into the so-called "cool crowd."

As long as this story reaches a single person, embracing them to turn their life around, my heart will be filled with joy and I know this book was well worth the hard work and dedication put into it.

Joseph Anthony Rivers
Los Angeles, 2010

# Introduction

12 years ago, I started my teaching career in Long Beach, California with the hopes that I would make a difference in the lives of my students. That first year would remain to be a special part of who I became as a teacher, so when it was time for that group of students to graduate from high school, I reached out to find them.

The first student I found was Joseph Rivers. I was thrilled to hear that, not only was he graduating, but he would soon move on to greater things. I can't say that I was surprised, because even as a 2nd grader, he already had plans of being successful. He already knew how to dream big. In a letter that was written at the end of that school year, Joseph wrote, "One day, I'll see you in the world somewhere." Little did I know that he would be seeing the world and sharing his story of how "All Great Things Begin with a Dream."

As I look back and wonder if I've made a difference in Joseph's life, I stop myself and realize that he's made a difference in mine. I couldn't be prouder of all that he has accomplished and I look forward to reading about where his dreams will take him.

Joy Bautista

*Joseph, I am proud to be apart of the village that is continuing to nurture you. I am excited to see many of the hopes and dreams you often shared with me in my office, are coming to fruition. Your current and future success comes from your commitment to excellence, your willingness to do the hard work and your passion to be the best. As I have always told you, "On your journey of self-discovery remember to take your time and enjoy the experience."*

Love, Mrs. Candyce Simpson
Jordan High School, Long Beach

*"A different kind of Guidance Counselor!"*

---

*Since the day I met Joseph he has always articulated his motivation to do well in school and be successful. My colleagues referred to Joseph, fondly, as "my adopted son" and wished they could have him as their adopted son. I want to attribute it to my counseling him however; I must say by all means, it was not my counseling but Joseph's charisma and attitude regarding his own goals. If anyone were to look for Joseph during his high school days they would find him either in my office or in the library working on his homework or his next school assignment. I feel like Joseph set the tone for tutoring at Jordan High School. In my ten years at Jordan I have never seen so many students stay after school or lunch to attend "math" tutoring. I had a college aide who was excellent in math, Joseph always came to see her, when other students saw Joseph getting help during lunch or after school they joined in as well.*

Stephanie Bilvado, Head Counselor
Lakewood High School

---

*When I think of Joseph Rivers I think of a leader. From the time I met him at Jordan High School I knew there was something amazing about him. I know that sounds cliche but it is really true. Joseph has a way of focusing himself and dedicating himself to what he wants. In an atmosphere such as Jordan High School it is not hard to see potential, but with Joseph it was something natural and innate.*

*He is the type of person that you absolutely enjoy and relish in whatever accomplishments he completes. You know and expect more of this young man and he demands the best. His dreams have always far exceeded his surroundings. From receiving the Bill Gates Scholarship and going to the school of his dreams and his most recent feat, "A Young Man with a Plan," Joseph Rivers is just getting started. I don't see him slowing down anytime soon, so the world should brace itself for amazing—*

Marquesa Lawrence, Career Counselor
Jordan High School, Long Beach

---

*Joseph Rivers is a man on a mission! From the time I met him when he walked into my junior English class; he has been working to change his life. As a public school teacher for the past 27 years, I have had the opportunity to work closely with thousands of kids and there are always those who leave an indelible impression on your mind. Joseph will be one of those I'll never forget. He worked hard to fill in the gaps in his learning so that he could be admitted to and survive in competitive colleges. He looked at the situation life had dealt him and strove to make it better. He desired to understand what it took to succeed, and he went after it—always with a smile on his face. I am proud of his accomplishments and know that he will continue to leave his mark as his life journey takes him in new directions.*

Sabrina Arney
AIMS Lead Teacher

---

*I'm very proud of Joe and liken his progress to a quiet storm. His diligence and humbleness have been a constant since I met him in 9th grade. Congratulations Joe on your project.*

Patrice Rice
High School Teacher

---

# 1
## Born into Misery

On October 14, 1990, I was born into the cold world as Joseph Anthony Rivers, also known as Joe Joe to my loving mother who cared deeply for me and my eldest sister, Starnisha. Three months after birth, my mother passed away and I had no answers as to what caused the mysterious death.

We lived on Johnson Street, one of the biggest drug-trafficking streets in the city of Compton. My father was known as one of the major dope dealers in the city. He was the least responsible and most unreliable individual you could ever meet. After dropping out of high school, he resorted to the streets, using the only skills he had ever acquired, survival skills. My father believed that he had no other purpose in life than to hustle, sell drugs, and make money.

However, my father was not in the drug business alone. He had several accomplices, including an uncle of mine who I knew I never wanted to be like. To make this situation worse, the drug deals all took place at the home where I lived.

The home was divided into three sections. At the very front of the property, there was a main house where my grandmother, grandfather, uncle, and I lived. Sometimes, my father would stay at the house, crashing on the couch. Located behind the front home were two separate houses where my two aunts and their families lived.

Each night I would lay my head down on my soft, cushioned pillow and I would hear all the voices that circled the dark alleys around my home. When I was 6 years old, I became very curious and decided to listen to what those voices were actually saying. I heard a female voice softly say, "Joe, you got that 'caine?"

I quickly awoke, as it was a little past midnight, and ran to the window as if the voice was speaking to me. Instead, I saw my father standing in the backyard with a lady who was unknown to me. I blankly stared at my father and watched as he pulled a small, plastic bag out of his pocket filled with what looked like white powder. My father then smiled slowly saying, "This that good cocaine. You will never find any other like this."

I then caught a glimpse of the unknown lady. She was the same person I'd seen standing on the corner, begging for change. It made me very angry to see her there. Many times I would ask my grandmother, "Why doesn't she get a job?" Grandmother would sweetly reply, "Pray for her and ask God to help her."

I then began to focus my eyes on the lady as she dug deep into her pocket. Seconds later, she pulled out a handful of money and handed some of it to my father and roughly placed the rest back into her pocket.

"Thanks and I'll be back," the lady said.

"No problem. You know where to find me," my father replied.

As the lady staggered away through the side gate to leave, my father cautiously looked to make sure her exit was successful. He returned into the house quietly, pulling the door shut.

I quickly jumped from the window and into my bed, thinking about what I had just seen and with questions swirling in my mind. What is cocaine? Why is my dad selling it? What does he do with the money?

With so many thoughts in my mind, I couldn't sleep. Instead, I kept envisioning the words my dad said to the lady. "This that good cocaine," kept playing in my head.

Seconds later, the door creaked open. I began to shake hastily because I thought my dad saw me spying on his transaction. But instead, it was the soft voice of my grandmother.

"Are you okay, baby? Do you need anything?" she asked.

I softly shook my head and said, "Can I come in the room with you and Papa?"

"Of course, let's go," my grandmother said.

At this moment, I debated whether I should tell my grandmother what I had just seen in her backyard, but I decided not to because I knew she would confront my father even if it meant getting physical. I also knew that my grandmother didn't agree with the type of business my father was involved in. I knew this because of the prior arguments and confrontations, each situation having the same concept of disagreement. I remember the first time I heard my grandmother speak of the situation about my father's bad habits.

"I don't agree with what you do, Joseph. Dope dealing is not an appropriate occupation when you have two children at stake and your babies' mother is gone, dead from this world," my grandmother said.

"This is who I am and it's what I do and I do not intend to change for anyone. This is how I was taught to make the funds to get what you need," my father shouted.

My grandmother would then tell my father to leave to avoid beating him lifeless.

My grandmother was a very strong individual who always did whatever it took to make sure the family was happy. The entire family called my grandmother "Mama" because she played a mother role to everyone. Mama was employed at the post office and believed that with hard work and dedication, anything was possible. However, she was a fighter and would do what she had to do in order to protect her family at all cost. She was always called a perfectionist and a workaholic because of how clean, organized, and focused she was at every task at hand. Since birth, Mama and I had a distinct relationship. She meant the world to me, so much that I referred to her as Mom. I felt I could tell her anything, trusting her with my life. But there was one thing Mama didn't play with, and that was education. She believed education was the meal-ticket to success, giving you the opportunity to be anything you want to be.

So as we proceeded to my grandparents' bedroom, I cautiously looked into the living room to find my dad lying down on the couch as if he had been there all night. A big question then popped into my head at that moment. What if Mama knows what my father is doing and just isn't saying anything? But then I began to realize that she would not purposely put—not only me, but the family in harm's way, so I released those thoughts immediately. As I laid there in bed with Papa and Mama, I began to feel a sense of comfort and protection as if I were Superman, made of steel, invincible to everything. I slowly began to close my eyes as Mama's right arm comforted my soul, holding me preciously.

I awoke the next morning, reminding myself that it was Sunday and this time was meant for church. However, my mind began to think about all of the incidents that took place the previous night. I quickly looked to see if my grandmother was still lying beside me, but she wasn't. Instead, lying next to me was grandfather, still sound asleep.

Now my grandfather wasn't the joyful, loving, caring, and honest type of grandfather. In fact, it was clear to see where my father got his evil and selfish characteristics from. Fortunately, those traits hopped past me. I knew right from wrong and my conscience threatened me deeply when I would head toward the wrong direction. Growing up, I use to say to myself—"Maybe Papa killed his good conscience."

My grandparents had been going through trials and tribulations even before my birth. My grandfather was very abusive and believed that it was his way or the highway. He was also the biggest adulterer in town and everyone knew not to mess with his operations or there would be consequences. Not only was he a cheat, but he was one of the top, retired drug dealers in the city, respected by all. In addition, he was the president of one of the most powerful motorcycle clubs in the city of Los Angeles, known as the Deuces'. With this powerful position came a lot of responsibility which was very time-consuming and involved a lot of women. My grandfather would constantly bring women to our home when my grandmother wasn't there. However, 80 percent of the time, she would catch him. When this happened, I knew what to expect and they knew the words that were going to be said.

First, the argument from the two would be very loud and fully composed of dreadful language—then, the physicality of my grandmother striking my grandfather. He would then grow angry at the accusations and began to beat my grandmother by punching her until she would go unconscious.

So as I stared at my grandfather on that bed, the first thought that came to mind was to get off that bed as quickly as possible. I did not like to be alone in the same room with him, so I jumped from the tall bed and I began to be guided to the kitchen by the pleasant scent of a freshly-cooked breakfast. The smell of my grandmother's pancakes, eggs, bacon, sausage, ham, and biscuit only made my stomach excited.

As I entered the kitchen, my grandmother was standing there, singing along to her gospel music. She was a stronger believer in God and attended church and bible study faithfully and was also a part of the choir.

As I walked over to the table, my grandmother firmly patted me on the head saying, "How did you sleep, baby?"

I quickly took my seat replying, "Just fine, Mama."

She then began to make my plate. She knew exactly how I liked my food and what to put on my plate. I then heard the front door open and a couple of seconds later, my father appeared.

"Good morning. Smells good in here. What you cooking, Mama?" my father asked.

"I'm making a Sunday breakfast before we go to church, somewhere you need to be," my grandmother replied.

I began to chuckle and grin because my grandmother was known for letting my father have it.

"You know I might just come down there and surprise you, Mama," father responded.

I quickly commented, "Yeah right."

My father then sat down next to me at the table. I wanted to get up so badly, but I didn't want my grandmother to think I was being rude.

My grandmother knew how I felt about my father. She knew that I did not like his ways and the activities he participated in, especially his drug deals that were happening more frequently. My grandmother was the only one who I spoke to about my father's questionable behavior.

"Hey, Joe. How you doing?" My grandfather suddenly appeared.

"I'm good. How you doing, Big Slick?" father replied.

"I'm good. Been busy at the club making sure my bikers okay," my grandfather said.

"That's alright with me, Slick. I see you still at it," father said.

"Yeah, you know me. By the way, we're having a party down at the club this Tuesday. You should come check it out," my grandfather said.

I quickly ate my food, trying to block out this conversation. Grandmother was still cooking in the kitchen, rejoicing, and singing loudly. I finished my plate, then got up quickly from the table and began to walk towards the kitchen.

"Ay, boy! You can't speak?" a voice said just as I was exiting the dining room.

"Hey. Good morning, Grandfather," I blankly said. I didn't even turn around to catch a glimpse of his face, and I continued to proceed to the kitchen.

"Hey, Mama. I'm done with my plate. This food was really good," I said.

"Thank you, I knew you would like it. Now go get dressed before we're late for church," grandmother said.

As I began to get dressed, I began to think about the similarities between my grandfather and father. They were both individuals I never wanted to be like.

"Joe Joe, let's go! We're late!" my grandmother yelled quickly, grabbing my attention.

My grandmother and I arrived at church, which was about 4 miles from the house. My grandmother would always speak to the people outside of the church before we would make our entrance. Once inside, we would sit on the left side of the congregation in the fifth row.

Church was something that I loved for two main reasons, the love that I had for inspirational singing and the significant message that came to me when listening to the preacher's sermon. I couldn't quite put my finger on how it happens, but every Sunday when I went to church, the Pastor would say something that related to my daily life which I would connect with on a spiritual level. That Sunday, I knew the Pastor's message would change my life forever.

"To all my youths, you can be anything you want to be in life. Nothing is impossible, for with hard work and dedication, you will see success. So never let anyone, and I mean anyone, limit your success, aspirations, dreams, goals and most of all, your faith," Pastor quoted.

# 2
## Incapable Father

Months began to pass by as I began to focus more on my father's mysterious activities. At this point my father and uncle had acquired many dope-feigned customers that would stop by the house feigning for the deadly drugs that were being slung on a regular basis. Everyone in the city knew where to go if they wanted the good drugs.

I began to question myself asking, "Why do they have to sling their products here around our home."

I never really got an answer but stayed curious of what was the purpose of selling drugs. I felt that there were other ways to obtain money; like working in a store, or fixing things, being a teacher, etc.

I also began to wonder where the money went that father earned because he had nothing to show for it. He never supported me or my sister monetarily or even physically. Father was so caught up into his own life that he rarely appeared in the life of his children's and in return we rarely appeared in his.

Father always made promises that would always end up making me resent him more and more. In my eyes he only cared about himself. There were many days that father would tell me that he would either be at a certain place or do something for me. It's sad to say at only age six I had that hatred in my heart in regards to my father which persuaded me to lose all trust in him.

It wasn't until October 14, 1997 that I discovered enough was enough and that my father didn't deserve another chance at that father-son bond.

"Hey grandma do you think he will come today," I excitedly exclaimed.

"I called him and he said he will be here, you know how your father is baby," Grandmother said.

"Yeah, I know, but today *is* my birthday and there are no excuses, he promised me he would get me the new *007* game but all I really want is him at my party mama." I said

"Well, look baby I don't want you to get your hopes to high because I hate when he lets you down, some people just never change baby, you listening?" Grandmother softly said.

"Yeah, I'm listening but it's my birthday, every birthday you always tell me it's my day and this is all I want, is for him to notice me." I sadly explained.

"Okay baby I understand, now give grandma a hug and I love you sweetie." Grandmother whispered in my ear as she hugged me.

Grandma then began to release me and as her eyes connected with mine I softly whispered back, "Some people do change and he will be here."

Grandma nodded her head in agreement and quietly proceeded into the kitchen.

It was noon and many people had called me to say those two exciting words, "Happy Birthday!" But there was still no call from my father yet. As I started to focus more on the thoughts of father not attending my birthday I began to get angry. I quickly released the anger by coming up with a solution for why he hadn't called or arrived. The best solution that I came up with was that it was too early; which sounded even ridiculous to me.

Although, this wasn't a solution but an excuse, I needed something to believe to calm my thoughts from being clustered with frustration.

As I sat in the living room with my favorite cousins Raymond, Halle, and Antowaniece discussing my birthday and what exactly I would be doing on that day someone began to hammer on the door.

I quickly jumped up shouting, "Told you mama, told you mama, he's here."

I ran for the door full speed leaving the rest of the family in the living room. As I got to the front door I began to shout, "Who is it" but stopped in the middle of the statement because I wanted to savior the moment of seeing my father's face.

I quickly turned the two security knobs on the door to the left to unlock it and then grabbed the door knob. Anxious and excited I swung the door open to see the beautiful face of my Aunt Thea.

Thea was my mother's sister, the mother of my closest cousin Raymond, and was the daughter of grandmother. She was known in the family for being the tough or strict aunt. She was the aunt who would punish you when you misbehaved with the powerful whopping method. Although, she had a reputation to be the punisher she was very loving and concerned not only about her immediate family but showed concern for the whole family. When I looked at her she reminded me of a superhero because she was the one to run to the aid of the majority of the family when anyone was being faced with a problem or physicality meaning as I would say, "Auntie Thea can fight." Aunt Thea always tells me of how I remind her of my mother and how she had her sister's back through everything. Aunt Thea and my mother had a very strong connection. From the various stories told to me by my aunt it seemed to me that Aunt Thea played more of a mother role to my mother which was something I considered sacred in their relationship.

"Hey Aunt Thea," I excitedly exclaimed

"Happy birthday, birthday boy; give auntie kiss," Aunt Thea said.

Then I noticed a shiny red box behind auntie's back that had an evenly placed red bow on it.

"What's in the box auntie?" I said.

"You will find out when you open your presents," Aunt Thea said.

I quickly grabbed the presents and rushed back to the table. As I began to place the beautifully wrapped presents upon the table I began to wonder where my father was. I then began to try to get him off of my mind but it didn't seem to work.

Time began to progress and father still wasn't there as afternoon began. At that point I didn't care if father came or not now because I felt as a father he should have been the first person there to arrive. That's one thing about me, I wouldn't say that I'm picky or moody but I have a big problem when people make a commitment or promise and fail to adhere to it. However, time continued to creep past me with every hour only guarantying a sense of emptiness as I sat their pretending to be happy playing with my cousins.

At that moment in time I froze and looked around the room and looked at my entire family. I noticed they were happy and that everyone came there to for me. This is when I noticed I had the ability to hide my true feelings to put on a sort of invisible mask to not show my true pain. Because deep down inside I wanted to burst into tears because I just wanted to believe that father would come so bad.

Grandmother had asked several times were I ready to cut the cake but I keep insisting that we wait for father. Then a friend of the family by the name of Tanya said the most staggering sentence I had ever felt in my young life.

"That damn Joe doesn't do anything right and I don't know why Joe Joe keep putting faith in him like he's going to change, that doesn't make Joe Joe any smarter than his damn daddy," Tanya whispered.

At that moment I just wanted everyone to leave but that invisible mask made me hold my composure for the family. I slowly stood up and walked over to grandmother peering at Tanya and alerted grandma that I wanted to cut the cake and get it over with. Grandmother knew at that moment that something was on my mind but I repeatedly assured her it was nothing.

"Can everyone come over here? It's time to cut my baby's cake!" Grandmother shouted.

Everyone began to circle around the kitchen table so I forced the biggest smile that would relay a message to everyone that I was happy. Aunt Thea then counted down and everyone began singing happy birthday. As I looked at the big vanilla frosted cake with the red words printed, Happy Birthday Joe Joe, I began to ask myself why I can't have a normal family. A definition of a normal family to me was having a mother and father like in the movies and what all my friends and family had. I then began to ask myself what is my purpose? Why am I here? Why would God take the parent that would have cared for me and left the one that doesn't?

None of my questions were answered in this short amount of time as my family continued singing happy birthday. So I began to focus back on reality just in time to hear grandmother telling me to make a wish. I slowly closed my eyes and bowed my head and silently whispered, "Lord please make father notice me and come to my party." I then lifted my head and blew out the candles to hear my family cheering. I then began to cut the cake with Aunt Thea's muscular hands gripping my arm to help me. I slowly began to visualize it was father but it only made more anger arise.

Time prolonged and everyone now had their cake and ice cream, danced, played games, and now it was time to open the presents. Before I could even mention opening the presents grandmother made a public announcements stating I would now open my presents. I felt like once again grandmother had some type of psychic ability that allowed her to know what I was thinking.

So once again my family crowded around the table in curiosity of the actions that I would display as I open my presents. So once again I portrayed that character who strives for happiness and peace and I smiled and thanked everyone gracefully for each present that I unwrapped. I then began to move for the shiny red box that accompanied Aunt Thea. As I held it I began to shake it around to try to get some sort of clue to satisfy my curiosity of its uniqueness. With no hint of what was in the box I began to rip open the shiny wrapping paper to see a black box that resembled a show box. With my interest flaring I quickly removed the top of the box to see the *007* game that father was suppose to bring. I then slowly raised my head and looked into Aunt Thea dark brown eyes and told her thank you. I could not ruin the family's rare moment of rejoice with any of my problems so I continued to hold on to my hurt and pain determined not to let anyone know my true feelings. But as I looked at grandmother she peered back into my eyes releasing a tear of her own. At that time I knew that father wasn't coming to my birthday party and that I wasn't important to him. I knew that he cared nothing for me. However, I did learn new things about myself. I learned that I had the ability to look inside myself and be strong even when filled with pain. I had the ability to hide my true feelings to make it seem like nothing affected me.

I got down to the very last present and saw that it said from grandma. So as I opened it I began to smile at her looking in her eyes. Grandmother was very historical as she smiled down upon me. I then ripped the last piece of wrapping from the box and threw the wrapping paper to the floor. I then froze as I held in my hands a children's storybook called *Hero*. My younger cousins' began to laugh but I knew this was the most meaningful present that I had received. However, this was no ordinary book; this book contained a photograph of my mother as she was pregnant with me on the front as if it had been cut to be the original illustration for the book. I hopped up, ran to grandmother and quickly hugged her, telling her how much I had loved and thanked her. The family then began to dance and shout, parading around the house. At this moment I grabbed grandmother close and looked into her soft eyes admitting to her that she was right, some things never change.

# 3
# Raids

At this point all the sweet and pleasant memories of my family being happy and blissful were just memories. After heavy consideration I began to believe that my family only reunited; showing love and affection on birthdays and family oriented events. This was because of the troubles and physicality's that constantly began to persist only months after me becoming 7 years of age.

It was on a cold Friday night that I just knew something bad was lurking. That same night, sirens and searchlights flashed around my home, and the streets were filled with police officers. Johnson Street was being raided from door to door in search of drugs and weapons. At only 7 years of age you could only wonder the feelings that were being driven through my head. As I peered out the window it seemed as if everything and everybody was moving in slow motion as the authorities cautiously preceded to knocking doors in and letting canines run free to aid them in their search. I knew it was just a matter of seconds until they would be making a grand entrance knocking down our door. I began to count in my head 5-4-3-2-1 and right on "one" I heard a loud bang at the door followed by, "This is LAPD and we have a search warrant, you have 10 seconds to comply or we will enter by force." At this time I was in the hallway peering around looking into the living room. I then began to focus on everyone's actions. Grandmother was focused on making sure everyone was okay, mainly screeching, "Call Gene and see if he is okay and make sure he has nothing to do with this."

Now Gene is grandmother's only son and also known as a bad boy. Uncle Gene defines himself as a hustler who mainly focuses on women and money. Growing up I would always see him with different women throughout the week. Uncle Gene also had several children with different women, which would always bring drama. Uncle Gene also had a record high for kids in the family, having thirteen. Looking at Uncle Gene various situations always led me to the conclusion that he was someone I never wanted to be like. However, everyone else that resided in this part of town did. Although, he wasn't from a particular gang or crew, many gave him this great respect as if he were some type of leader. He was a one man army whom occasionally worked with my father on certain deals.

But to revert back to the storyline I then looked at my sister as her face displayed such a worried and lost feeling, as if she didn't know what to do. At this time another one of my aunts by the name of Freda stood next to grandmother at the front door, looking worried but at the same time filled with courage as she quoted, "We have nothing to hide."

Yes, it's amazing how my senses were working to capture all this in a matter of ten seconds which were given to us by the officer standing on the other side of the door with a battering ram. At the count of eight, Aunt Freda jerked the door open politely stating, "How may I help you officer."

The officer then aggressively told Aunt Freda to open the door; flashing the search warrant past the screen door. With the search warrant present this stood as an indication for Aunt Freda to open the door. Aunt Freda began to unlock the top chain and then the bottom two locks but before she could fully open the door police began to rush in screaming, "DOWN ON THE GROUND NOW!" in constant repetition. I quickly dived to the ground and looked around to see my other family members on the ground. However, grandmother stood there sitting on the couch as if this had happened before. The officers that had fluttered the house were still checking portions of it and even the two back houses were being searched, of which one belonged to my Aunt Freda and the other to Aunt Thea. At this time as I lay there on the floor I began to try to connect this to my father's mysterious actions. I then heard one of the officers say I'll check the backyard. From that moment I knew something wasn't right. Why was the backyard being targeted? My curiosity choked within me instantly, as I peered at the officers from my ground view of the backyard. My mind then went into a kind shock as I saw a search dog began to dig as if it found something of importance. But what could be that important? What could be in our yard that has drawn so much attention from the local authorities? I didn't know but I was sure in a couple of seconds I would find out. The search dog then began to pull a clear bag from the small hole dug.

As I gazed with curiosity I caught a clear glimpse of the bag which seemed to be filled with a white powdery content. The cop who seemed to be in charge then yelled to the officers, "We got it." However, I began to notice that the search wasn't over. The vicious beast began to snarl and mutter as its head dug deep into the ground. Seconds later the canine's head arouse from the ground nearly ripping several black trash bags. The officer then grabbed the torn bag from the canine, stuck his hand deep inside and pulled out several stacks of cash. The officer's eyes then gloomed as if they just had seen a ghost. I thought to myself maybe they were surprised by how much monetary value the trash bag contained. I then focused back onto the designated officer who had just given the okay to stand and be seated in the living room. As I stood to my feet, my eyes were still focused on the officers who were in the backyard as the search dog continued to dig through the ground. I slowly began to walk towards the living room not taking my eyes off of the officers in the backyard. Just as I got into the living room I saw the search dog pull out some sort of bottle shaped container which seemed to be filled with loads of coins with small inserts of cash in certain areas. I then regained focus as I gazed around the living room. Suddenly grandmother's voice caught my attention as she softly whispered, "Are you okay baby."

I quickly replied, "Yes Mama."

As I walked over to the plastic wrapped couch the officer told me I can sit next to grandmother on the couch and then insured me that everything will be okay. At this age I didn't understand a police officer's motive for just ramming into someone house. Actually,

I began to look at the local authorities as the bad guys; the ones who abused their power for unexcused reasons. Hey, but what do I know—I'm only seven years old. I slowly began to go off in another daze as everything became motionless as if time had frozen. I looked at Aunt Freda as her face showed such a worried concern as if something bad had happened or was going to happen. She knew something but I just couldn't quite figure it out based on a facial expression alone. I then slowly focused my senses on the couch. My sister's face showed a great amount of amazement and confusion as she sat there in awe looking at the floor. I then slowly focused my head to the right where grandmother was sitting. I then tried to analyze grandmother but was stopped when I seen the white powdery content compiled into a small bag. I knew this situation was serious at this point because it made me think back to the night when I spied on my father's transaction in which he acted cautious and paranoid; looking around not to be spotted as he passed that same small bag to the mysterious lady. I then regained my focus as the officer's deep voice slowly began to speak.

"So, my name is John Williams and I'm a part of the LAPD homicide unit in the city Compton and I'm going to explain why we were raiding the street and more particularly your home," Officer Williams said.

His look was very serious and he had a very straightforward tone in his voice.

"Firstly, we are investigating a murder that took place right around the corner. I would like to ask if any of you know anything about it." Officer Williams asked.

I looked to see if anyone would respond.

"We don't know anything about that officer and I can ensure you that no one in my household is involved with this situation," Grandmother responded.

The officer's look was very stern. I knew there was more to the story so I patiently waited to hear the rest.

"However, there is more to the story. We recently received information from several informants that this is one of the main drug operation locations," officer Williams explained.

Grandmother quickly interrupted with a loud WHAT!!!

"Let me finish Madam, from the gathering of information from our informants we have apprehended a possible suspect who was caught at the scene of the crime," Officer Williams said.

"That's great," I quickly said to myself.

"So where is this going? I have a feeling there's still more." Aunt Freda replied.

Officer Williams than took a deep breath.

"The suspect that we have apprehended is said to live here and is a relative to this family," Officer Williams explained.

Grandmother eyes exploded as I knew it was only seconds until she would comment.

"Officer Williams I don't know what is going on here but I would like to know who you guys have in custody," grandmother curiously explained.

My eyes then shifted to the kitchen where I had seen Officer Williams' partner walking toward the living room where we were having our discussion.

"Can I talk to you for a minute," the officer said.

Officer Williams then whispered to grandmother

to give him a sec. As the officers shared a discussion, grandmother and Aunt Freda shared one also.

"Who could they be talking about Mama," Aunt Freda asked.

"I don't know," grandmother replied.

I looked in the kitchen to see Officer Williams nodding his head, slowly walking back to the living room. As he returned to his seat he took yet another deep breath.

"Sorry to be the bearer of bad news but the relative of this family that we have in custody is Eugene Shallowhorn," Officer Williams explained.

# 4
## My Plan Starts Now

As the officers began to wrap up their investigation and exit the premises we sat there in the living room shocked and in awe. I began to look around the room to see everyone's reactions but before I could examine them grandmother began to speak.

"Can you repeat your last statement officer," grandmother asked.

Officer Williams took a deep breath before he replied.

"The suspect we have apprehended is Eugene Shallowhorn and he will be held in custody until this investigation is complete," Officer Williams replied.

I looked at grandmother and began to see tears fall from her eyes; I can tell this was what she was afraid of when she alerted Aunt Freda to call Uncle Eugene and make sure he had nothing to do with this.

I then focused my attention back on Officer Williams as he arose from his seat.

Grandmother quickly stated, "You know that's my son."

"I know Mrs. Shallowhorn, and that's why you have my word. I will let you know what's going on every step of the way as we go through this investigation. But I'm sorry we have to get back to work and any damages that may have been caused to your home by the LAPD will be reimbursed to you," Officer Williams promised.

As Officer Williams left the living room, we sat there silent as we thought about the shocking news. I then began to hear grandmother whimper in a tone that I was very familiar with. I arose from my seat and moved closer to her and put my arm around her. Whenever grandmother cried it was only a matter of time before I would begin to cry. I think this is where my vow to protect grandmother kicked in the most, when she cried. So as I sat there with my arm around her crying to her cries, I knew it was only seconds before she would try to be strong for me, placing her arm around me.

"It's okay baby, everything is going to be alright," Grandmother whispered in my ear.

As I sat there in grandmother's arms I began to pull my sister closer. She had begun to whimper in a low tone also. I then looked around for Aunt Freda. Seconds later she walked through the kitchen and back into the living room.

"The house is locked up Mama." Aunt Freda said.

Aunt Freda was always silent most of the time. Growing up and watching her I always came to the conclusion that she kept a lot of things inside. I then suddenly looked back at grandmother who had called my name several times to get my attention.

"It's time for bed Joe Joe and Starnisha," Grandmother said.

As I hopped into my bed I couldn't help but think that my dad had something to do with this. I even began to ask myself where he could be or why grandfather wasn't here. Seconds later my eyes began to close but opened later that night due to the sound of a low cry. I knew it was grandmother's cry. She had been up all night calling the Lynwood Correctional facility trying to get inmate information on Uncle Gene. From the tone of her voice I could tell the results were not coming back in her favor. I tried to think of ways I could be helpful in this situation but nothing came to mind. So I closed my eyes and returned to bed hoping that this would all become a dream and never happen.

The next morning I awoke and heard a big discussion in the kitchen. I quickly jumped out of the bed and tiptoed into the hallway so I can have a clear view into the kitchen unnoticed. Grandmother, Aunt Freda, Aunt Thea, Grandfather, and my father were all sitting at the table. It sounded to me as if they were trying to figure out exactly what happened and what they were going do about Uncle Gene. After a shared input of ideas, grandmother then started to speak in a loud tone discussing Uncle Gene's charges and court date. I can tell she was frustrated and stressed by the facial expressions that she made as she spoke. I knew this day was only going to get worse before it got better. After listening in to the conversation for several minutes I began to look at my father in disgust as he spoke. I noticed that each time I saw him I acquired more and more resentment toward him. I began to focus back onto the conversation and noticed that it was coming to an end. I quickly bounced up from the floor and into the bathroom. Seconds later there was a knock on the bathroom door followed by a gospel hymn which alerted me that it was grandmother.

I opened the door saying, "Good morning Mama."

"Good morning baby, are you hungry," Grandmother replied in a soft tone.

"No Mama, I'm fine," I said.

I continued to the kitchen not caring to be spotted anymore.

"Good morning everyone," I said.

I quickly walked through the kitchen not even listening to the family's response. As I got into the living room I headed straight towards the front door cautiously walking out after the events that took place last night. As I gazed into the Saturday sun I just began to think and look around at my environment. I began to think about all the nights it was hard to sleep not knowing if a shot would break through the wooden door and hit me or one of my relatives. I began to look at how the streets were filled with potholes and how violent people were. It seemed as if everyone lacked a purpose and dream. At such a young age I was able to tie the words purpose and dream together. I may have been ten but I knew my purpose was something so much more than the streets of Compton. I knew that it was time that I started to pay attention to my surroundings because the decisions I made from here on out would impact my plan. I knew from this point I would be criticized for being different or having dreams that surpassed the sky's limits. As I sat there gazing into the sky catching the peaceful breeze I began to feel a sense of comfort come across me. This comfort ensured me that the long road that I am destined to embark on will be filled with obstacles that will try to break not only my faith but also my courage. As I thought about this powerful message that crossed my mind, my eyes began to roam over to the tall palm trees in front of our home. The wind silently pushed the palm trees from side to side, bending them. As I sat there on the porch watching the palm trees I began to understand how my faith and courage would be tested as the wind blew harder and harder in an attempt to knock the palm trees down. I knew this was a message that signified that I would face devastating winds that would cause me to bend, but in those times I would have to find the courage within myself not to break.

*I knew that my plan had just begun.*

# 5
## Bad News

As weeks began to pass by we learned more and more about Uncle Gene's conviction. He had been to court several times and I was sure he would be there many more. I would sometimes try to eavesdrop on what was going on when the family spoke of Uncle Gene but only got confused because I didn't understand what certain things meant. However, I knew that what he was facing wasn't going to go away overnight. In addition, I noticed grandmother becoming weaker with each series of unfortunate events. This made me sad because I knew that I would have to step up and portray the comforter to keep grandmother going. It also made me angry because grandmother didn't deserve any of what she was going through.

As I lay there in my bed gazing up at the ceiling I began to wonder what may lie ahead. I knew that this situation had already caused a lot of heartache. But I knew that I would have to stay strong for my grandmother because I was the light that kept her persevering as she was mine's.

No one will ever understand the visions that lay in my mind at such a young age. But I knew they empowered me to stay persistent, reaching for the next vision. Ultimately, these visions not only acted as my senses but also my guide.

As time progressed I began to pay closer attention to all the conversations that took place in my home. This helped me learn what was going on with Uncle Gene and how the legal system functioned. Even so that I began to research the words that I overheard such as trial, prosecutors, juries, and even suspects in a dictionary that was given to me by my 2nd grade teacher. So when I heard grandmother say that Uncle Gene's trial date was set for tomorrow I knew what to expect, although I was expected not to know.

One side of my soul supported my Uncle Gene.

But one side questioned if he was getting what he deserved.

I quickly awoke to the loud alarm clock that awakened my sister and me. I knew that it was time to get ready for the trial hearing. As I brushed my teeth I stared into the mirror before I would gargle to rinse my mouth.

Suddenly I began to see a vision filled with pain as grandmother screeched loudly followed by loud clinging bars. I wondered what this could mean. I sat in the bathroom trying to examine the vision or replay it but failed on both accounts due to a loud interference of someone knocked on the door.

"I'm coming now, give me a sec. I'll be right out," I quickly responded.

I opened the door and slowly raised my eyes to meet the eyes of grandmother.

"Good thing you're up baby. Now I can go ahead and get dressed," grandmother said.

I could see pain in grandmother eyes. I could see that she was reserving herself to appear fine to the family. As she went into the bathroom I proceeded to the kitchen to grab a bite to eat. When I entered the kitchen I was surprised to see most of the family up and ready to go. Everyone seemed quiet as if they were thinking about the situation and how it would turn out. I continued on to make a sandwich but stopped when my curiosity hit me with a question.

"Have you seen my dad, grandfather?" I softly said.

"Nope I don't know where he is. He should've of been here by now," grandfather replied.

Oh well, I thought to myself.

Faith was something I always believed in although I had no idea what the word meant. But I knew the faith that I had once put into loving my father was gone. At ten years of age I knew that my father cared nothing about me or my sister. But I wanted to see how deep the rabbit hole would go. So I made a vow that I would endure and forgive until I can one day build up the courage to ask the most pertinent question ever.

Why?

After eating my breakfast grandmother came rushing down the hallway alerting everyone that it is time to go. I quickly got into the car and then lent a helping hand to my younger cousin Raymond.

"Where's Aunt Thea, Raymond?" I said.

He lifted a finger and pointed at the car behind us which contained Aunt Thea, Aunt Freda, and their husbands.

"Fasten your seatbelt," grandmother said as she peered back from the front seat.

Grandfather then started the engine and continued to the local courthouse in Compton.

Upon arrival I peered into the front seat to catch grandmother reciting a small prayer followed by a deep sigh. I can tell this prayer was significant to grandmother because her head remained bowed much longer than usual. I begin to wonder what could she praying for.

Is it protection? Guidance? Love? Support? Whatever it was you can tell grandmother meant it.

The car then came to a complete stop as I anxiously opened the door and hopped out of the car stretching immediately. Seconds later I heard the car door slam behind me. I turned around quickly to see grandmother fixing her blouse and beginning to walk towards the building. As we began to walk towards the courthouse I began to ask grandmother several questions trying to figure out as much information about the justice system before we got into the courtroom where there would be complete silence.

"So what is going to happen today, grandmother," I said.

"Your Uncle Gene's case will be discussed. After the discussion the judge will make a decision if he is either guilty or not guilty," grandmother replied.

"Good thing I researched all those court terms," I muttered to myself.

We then finally made our way to the entrance of the Compton courthouse which was filled with people exiting and enter the facility. We then went through several metal detectors and eventually up the flight of escalators that would lead us to room 219B where the trial was being held.

Suddenly the vision of grandmother screaming loudly followed by clinging bars played in my mind once again. Why was I constantly having this vision? Was someone trying to tell me something?

We reached 219B and quietly entered. The trial hadn't begun but everyone was patiently sitting in the wooden seats. Grandfather guided the family into two rows at the front of the room right behind my Uncle Gene's attorney. I remembered my Uncle Gene's attorney because every time he came to our home he would give me a Lollipop and grandmother would always say, "Tell Mr. King, thank you." Grandmother was very still and quiet only speaking to greet Mr. King. I placed my hand on top of hers to let her know she had my support and comfort.

After minutes passed by with only whispers floating throughout the courtroom, the door on the right side of the courtroom opened and the jury began to make their entrance; twelve in total. Minutes later the officer standing at the front of the courtroom gave a command for everyone to stand. I couldn't quite hear what he said but I arose from my seat so I would not be the only one still sitting. After announcing the judge whom would be handling the trial, he gave the audience the command to be seated.

I heard the door creak open and looked back to see my dad entering the courtroom. He walked to the front of the courtroom and sat next to me taking a seat on the edge of my seat. I looked at grandmother to see if she had noticed him here, however she was still in a daze with her eyes glued to the front of the room.

I quietly scooted closer to grandmother and held her tightly, rubbing her back. The judge began to speak and seconds later Uncle Gene came out of the back door in an orange outfit of some kind. He was handcuffed and escorted to his seat next to Mr. King. Grandmother eyes began to swell and I knew sooner or later this would sink in on her. Grandfather sat still at the end of the row with one arm around my sister Starnisha. The rest of the family sat patiently awaiting the judge's next words. The judge began to speak again this time speaking directly to Mr. King and Uncle Gene.

"How do you plea," the judge said.

"My client pleads not guilty, your honor," Mr. King responds.

"All right let the trial begin," the judge said.

The trial went on for hours and several witnesses had spoken when called to the stand. We had also went on a recess and returned, and on that recess I had learned that the family of the woman that was murdered was in this courtroom. In addition, Uncle Gene wasn't the only suspect that was being tried. In fact, there were two others that had already been tried and were given life sentences. This information scared me and made grandmother shed tears. By this time of the trial Aunt Thea had moved down several seats to sit on the other side of grandmother to console her. My father still sat next to me quietly listening to the judge and Aunt Freda held Raymond as he fell asleep. Suddenly, the judge made a loud announcement.

"Has the jury reached a verdict?" the judge said.

"Yes your honor, in the case of Gene Shallowhorn vs. the deceased Debrah Mills we find Gene

Shallowhorn guilty on all charges," the jury spokesman replied.

A loud gasp filled the courtroom, followed by thunderous cries. The audience then quickly became filled with mixed emotions. Some cried, while others applauded, but all was impeded by the large gavel that was banged against the stand by the judge.

"Sentencing will be in a week, meeting adjourned," the judge concluded.

She then banged the gavel one last time and then disappeared into the back room behind her stand. Uncle Gene turned to grandmother but right before he could speak he was pulled from his seat and escorted back into the door that he had come out of.

Suddenly a loud scream arose above all the noise. It was the same noise that I had been hearing in my vision. I looked to the left to see the family trying to comfort grandmother. Grandmother's cries caused my tears to run loose. I had never seen grandmother like this. She yelled and screamed why unto the Lord. I quickly began to grab the hand of grandmother softly reminding her it's going to be okay. At this time I don't know if she heard me or not but I wasn't going to give up. I needed grandmother. She was all I had left. Then the unthinkable happen, grandmother collapsed and went unconscious.

Kim Shallowhorn, mother of Joseph Anthony Rivers, as a teenager.

From left to right—Ronald Tribble, Darrell Pope, Eugene Shallowhorn and Joseph Rivers, father of Joseph Anthony Rivers.

Kim Shallowhorn as a teenager.

Alfred Shallowhorn and his granddaughter Starnisha Rivers.

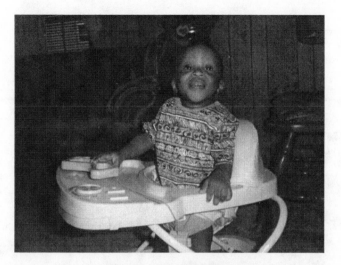

**Joseph Anthony Rivers**

**With family friend Curtis Simmons.**

**The Shallowhorn women—Thea (far left), Kim (middle),
Freda (back middle) and Edna (far right).**

**Edna and Alfred Shallowhorn**

**5th Grade Class, Joseph Anthony Rivers is at the far left.**

Edna Shallowhorn, grandmother of Joseph Anthony Rivers.

# 6
## Alone, but Saved by a Teacher

I'm all alone and I never thought this day would come. The one person whom was not just my strength but "my everything" was removed from my life within a matter of moments. Grandmother was taken to the local hospital after the trial. She began to have a nervous breakdown, which later turned into seizures. Doctors feared that she would never be the same and would have to be taken care of. This also meant that I would have to be taken care of by someone other than grandmother. It made me sad when I wondered who would step up to care for me. Grandfather couldn't take care of me because his personal life was far more important than tending to a child and my aunties had families of their own. At least these were my opinions of the reasons I may have been be a burden on them. Shockingly, my father convinced the family that he was fit to take care of my sister and I and we were shifted into his care.

In this part of the book you will learn that sometimes you have to find motivation deep within yourself when you feel all hope is gone. It's always easy to give up but it takes real strength to overcome the obstacles you fear most.

After moving with my father I became very reserved and kept to myself. Although, we had a complete family which consisted of my father, my sister, my stepmother, my older brother, my younger brother and myself, I felt incomplete. I couldn't help but feel I did not belong. The only place that satisfied my emptiness to be with grandmother was school. There I felt I had a piece of her with me as I remembered her word softly explaining how important education was. However, I had no one to talk to about how I felt, or what I was experiencing. I had to learn to cope with my situations and find happiness through the pleasant memories that lay deep inside my soul.

As weeks passed, I rarely spoke to grandmother and when I did it was very brief. She always sounded sick as she asked how I was doing. I can tell she missed me just as much as I missed her because she would always end the conversation by saying, "Be strong and I love you baby." These words gave me the strength to carry on.

I awoke early the next morning anxious to get to school because it was the day that the students would present their projects to the class. The projects that we were going to present focused on helping us determine our dreams and steps to achieve them. My dreams were always big, such as being a doctor, going to the NBA, or being a famous author and always involved giving back to others, so I knew this project wouldn't be too hard for me. I actually thought that this project would be rather fun. I would always get very nervous before presenting it in front of the class but my second grade teacher Ms. Bautista always made me feel comfortable when speaking.

Ms. Bautista was my second grade teacher and the person that I would talk to on a more personal level about my problems. She seemed to listen and truly cared not just about my well-being but my future. I felt I could trust her so I became emotionally attached to her—viewing her as my mentor. On most school days I would stay after class sometimes just listening to her lectures on the importance of education. She helped shaped my dream and empowered my will to succeed.

Minutes had passed by as Ms. Bautista continued to speak on who would go first. I had gotten a funny feeling that she would call me in a matter of seconds. After presenting several presentations in Ms. Bautista's class I knew that she used my work as a sort of an example.

"Joseph R. you will be going first," Ms. Bautista said.

I was called Joseph R. because there was three Joseph's in my class including myself. In addition, Joseph Z. was my best friend while in elementary school.

Right after Ms. Bautista finished speaking on the order of presentations and what she expected; she pointed a finger at me to come to the front of the class. I slowly grabbed my poster board and my sheet of paper which contained the storyline for my poster. As I walked to the front of the class, everyone's eyes and attentions became focused on me. I looked down at my hand to see if it was shaking but ironically it was still. I made my way to the front of the class in which I first scanned my audience. Some students were in their own world and some were waiting patiently for me to speak. I took a deep breath and looked at Ms. Bautista waiting for the indication to start.

"Good morning class, my name is Joseph and the title of my project is "Big Dreams Do Come True." When I grow up I want to be a doctor. I would like to be a doctor because I like to help people that are hurt or need help. To accomplish my dreams I plan to go to college so I can be trained to do so. I will show the world that big dreams do come true with hard work."

After presenting the storyline I showed the class my illustration which showed me in a hospital room taking care of a patient. In the illustration I was dressed in a white lab coat with a badge on my coat that said Dr. Rivers.

After showing my illustration I looked at Ms. Bautista to see her smiling and silently cheering. I then focused back on the class to see if there were any questions. After a couple seconds of silence I quietly began to walk back to my seat as the class clapped and tried to whistle.

Ms. Bautista then came back up to the front of the class to speak in which she explained that our projects should be presented like mine's. She then called the next student up to the front of the classroom and began to walk over to my desk. She bent down next to me and marked a big "A" on the top of my paper with a red marker.

"Good job, Joseph it was excellent," said Ms. Bautista.

After class I normally chatted with Ms. Bautista about things other than class such as problems and concerns that I had been feeling. She often offered encouragement and motivation which gave me strength to overcome whatever obstacles that lay in my path. So I knew once that bell rang in the next 3 minutes I would have a long talk about the problems I had been facing.

The bell rang and all the students rushed out of the classroom excited to be free. I knew I had about 20-30 minutes until father would arrive in his large black truck to pick me up. I slowly arose from my seat after daydreaming and walked to the desk in which Mrs. Bautista was organizing.

"Do you have a minute to talk Ms. Bautista," I softly said.

I knew she would be interested in hearing what I had to say especially if it was bothering me.

"Yes, Joseph I always have time to talk. Anything you need to talk to me about feel free anytime," Ms. Bautista gently replied.

"Ms. Bautista, I don't live with my granny no more. The judge gave me back to my dad and I hate it there. Granny got really sick after my uncle went to prison. Everything is going wrong and I don't know what to do," I replied.

Before I knew it Ms. Bautista eyes started to water.

"You are going to be fine, Joseph. Don't let anything or anyone get you down. I know that things are hard for you now but you will overcome all of your obstacles. I know this because you are my most brightest student and there's something in you that you haven't discovered yet but I want you to be strong," Ms. Bautista softly said.

Right after those words I heard my named being screamed in the hallway. I quickly thanked Ms.

Bautista and told her I would never forget those words as I grabbed my things and began to run for the door.

"WAIT!! Joseph, here take some snacks with you," she yelled.

I ran back to her desk and grabbed the small Ziploc bag of graham crackers and the napkin full of Twizzlers. I then thanked her and took off for the door yelling HERE I COME!!

After making it down the hall my cousin Ronnie was their waiting for me.

"You alright?" Ronnie asked.

"Yeah, I was just talking to my teacher about some things," I replied.

Now Ronnie was one of my cousin's that I was always around because we were so close in age. He was two years older than me and kind of kept an eye on me during school hours. He was also the son of my Aunt Thea.

"I was just checking if you wanted to come out to the playground and play around for awhile until your dad gets here," Ronnie said.

"Yeah, let's go," I responded.

As we got to the playground we played on the jungle gym running around and climbing the gray metal bars several times until reaching fatigue. I then went to the benches behind the basketball courts and took a seat there until I was able to catch my breath. After catching my breath I began to look down at the pavement when a bright orange basketball came rolling to my feet. I picked it up and dribbled to the courts preparing to shoot. After taking the first shot I heard a loud engine flare. I knew this roaring sound meant it was almost time for me leave.

I always hated the sound of that engine. Maybe it was because it was an indication that I would have to return back to a place that I did not want to be.

After telling my cousin I was about to leave I heard the horn honk two times. "I'll see you tomorrow Ronnie and if you see granny tell her to call me." I said.

He shook his head in agreement and I turned around and started to walk toward the truck.

I knew that by telling my cousin to tell grandmother to call me would probably be the only way I would talk to her. When I was at father's home I didn't even feel comfortable using the phone unless no one was there.

After getting to the truck I turned around to see all the kids still playing on the playground.

"Get in the car Joe Joe," father said.

I opened the large black door and threw my bag on the seat and slowly climbed into the truck. After closing the door I started to buckle my seatbelt and the car pulled off. Whenever I got into the truck there was no father-son conversation. He never once asked me how was school? Or how was your day? However, there was always a soft jazz tone that was being played in the car.

After driving miles I thought I would break the silence so I turned to father trying to think what to ask.

"Joe, where's Starnisha?" I asked.

He looked at me in sort of a shock as if I had done something wrong so I quickly turned my head to hide from what he would say next.

"You don't call me Joe—you either call me dad, pops, or father something. I don't see how you can call everyone else by their name but call me Joe. But it's okay, we gonna fix that," father replied.

I didn't understand how he can just expect me to be the loving son when I barely know who he was. Sure he's my father but he rarely came around. He missed all of my most memorable events. I can't explain why I couldn't call him by a name that symbolized he was a father, but it just didn't feel right coming out of my mouth. However, I knew I would have to be strong at all times and never show any weakness. So I knew I would have to acquire a hobby that would allow me to release my anger, happiness, sadness, obstacles and most importantly the true feelings that lay within my heart, although my actions displayed otherwise. So as my father and I made our way home I silently opened my backpack, reached my hand deep inside, and pulled out a notebook and pen. I then began to write.

# 7
## Perseverance, Faith, & Honesty

Writing became not only a way to free my mind but something I actually enjoyed doing. Writing was that motivation inside of me that acted as an aid which kept me persevering through my obstacles.

"Perseverance" is defined as persisting in spite of difficulties. This was the first definition I learned. Not because I wanted to but because it symbolized me. It symbolized who I was and what great strength I had through my intellect. As your reading this book you may have many questions as I had. You may be confused as I was. But this is the road I have to pursue to bring you into my world. Grandmother used to always say to me, "You will never understand a person until you walk a mile in their shoes." Well, prepare to take that mile. But be assured you will not be taking the walk alone because there is something called faith that lies within each of us.

This was the hardest chapter for me to write. I had to relive all the feelings I thought were gone to bring out the true emotion inside of me. I have no regrets and hold no grudges but I learned to cope and how to find myself with the help of a plan.

The plan itself was not something that was

originated based on vengeance but success. If you think this story will get better at this moment you might want to turn back now but if you want to see just how much a young man can bare to accomplish his dreams keep reading forward.

Three years has passed and I'm now in the 5th grade. I stayed consistent when it came to education and made my mark as being a smart kid. At every assembly my friends knew I would receive honors. If you received a principal's honor you were one of the top students at my school. Over the years I met new friends and many wonderful teachers but Ms. Bautista was still the teacher I would run back to whenever I had something on my mind. However, she ended up leaving McKinley Elementary School in the middle of my 5th grade year. I was really sad because I felt I had no one to talk to about my problems or the way I felt so I was forced to bottle it all up inside.

Even though, I was still under the care of my father I got to interact with my family a little bit more over the years. It was nice to hear that they all moved off Johnson Street and more so out of the city of Compton. My aunts Thea and Freda moved to Long Beach which wasn't that far away, grandmother stayed with her mother in another part of Compton and honestly I don't know where grandfather was but I know he wasn't with my grandmother.

I really want you to pay attention to the definitions that you read from this point on because they all hold a specific component that will in the end equal how I achieved my success. Honesty is defined as free from deception or just truthful. Notice that I didn't give an exact location for grandfather's whereabouts. This symbolizes that before you can reach your full potential in life you have to be honest with yourself. Can you honestly say that you forgive someone in your life that has hurt you severely maybe emotionally or physically?

After the incident with Uncle Gene I guess everyone figured it was time to get off of Johnson Street. However, just because everyone resided in a new location didn't mean that conflict wouldn't follow. In fact, I think this is where it began.

I quietly awoke one morning happy to see the bright sun shining in my face—I was so happy that it was summer. I would not have to wake up early and the best part about it was that I would get to be with grandmother more often. Being around grandmother really made me sad because she still wasn't fully well—she didn't have the breakdowns as much but she did have seizures which constantly were active.

The first day I encountered one of grandmother's seizures was when I was at my great-grandma's house where grandmother resided.

Everyone called great-grandma "Big Mama," not because she was the eldest relative but because she was the most respected. One thing Big Mama hated was to see young adults with their pants sagging. She believed in an old-school tradition where you did not have to fit in with everyone.

So as my father pulled to the front of Big Mama's house I became excitedly happy to see grandmother. Father's foot stomped on the break and the big black truck came to a halt.

My father and I still had no father-son relationship even though it had been a little over 3 years. I mean we weren't strangers where we didn't speak at all but there was no bond. So getting out of the car I was not expecting him to say the words "have a nice day" or "I love you son" because I knew it wasn't going to happen.

So as I opened his door he continued to look forward as if he were still focusing on the road. Once again I decided to break the silence.

"Thank you, Joe," I said.

I knew he hated when I called him that name but it was the only name I knew for him. But I waited a couple of seconds to see if he would respond but instead he just turned his head away from me as if he was filled with disappointment. I jumped down from the truck and closed the door and begin to walk to the gate.

Right before I could open the gate I heard a voice say, "Joe, call me when you ready to come home."

I didn't even turn around to catch the look on his face as he said it but instead I continued through the gate.

Once I got to the front door Big Mama was at the door patiently waiting for me.

"How you doing baby, you alright? I haven't seen you in so long. Give me a hug baby," Big Mama said.

After greeting Big Mama I walked inside the house to greet the rest of the family. Big Mama's son James and two daughters, Marie and Margie, also resided in the home.

"Hello everyone," I shouted.

They all responded by standing up giving me hugs and telling me how proud they were of all my academic achievements.

Seconds later I heard a voice I was familiar with that I had been missing for some time now.

"Is that my baby? Awwww I heard you got a new award. The Presidential Honor signed by the president, baby." Grandmother said.

I became super excited once she said that because I had no idea she knew about the award.

"Yes Mama, I got the award and it was so cool I can't believe it. They gave it to me in a frame. All my friends were just looking like I already knew they were going to give me something big," I excitedly responded.

Before I knew it I had talked a good 20 minutes about all my achievements. It just felt good to tell the person who first fueled my commitment to education and all the wonderful achievements I accomplished.

"Joe Joe I have a present for you—wait right here," grandmother said.

The remaining family that was still in the living room looked on with grins on their faces as if they knew I would like what I was about to receive.

While grandmother was in the room fumbling boxes around I began to think how much better she looked. She looked as if she was happy and becoming well.

A second later grandmother returned from the bedroom with a huge box that was nicely wrapped.

"Here you go baby," grandmother said.

I quickly began tearing the wrapping paper while constantly thanking her for the present.

Once I got to the last piece of the wrapping paper hiding the surprise inside I smiled because I thought I had a clue of what it was. My hands began to get more excited as I saw what the present was.

"Ah yeah, this is so cool, a Nintendo 64 and two games. Thank you so much grandmother. I love you," I eagerly shouted.

"I love you too baby, now go have fun," grandmother replied.

I played for hours and hours until I grew fatigued and passed out on the bed.

"HELP! HELP!! Call 911 again," the voice said.

I quickly awoke after hearing that familiar voice. I ran to the living room prepared to protect grandmother with any means necessary.

Once I made it to the living room I was shocked to see no one being hurt but grandmother on the floor screeching loudly. Her brother and sisters were around her and Big Mama was calling 911. I quickly ran over to grandmother and budged my way through Aunt Margie to be as close as possible to her as I could to comfort her.

"MAMA! MAMA! You okay!?" I yelled.

I knew she heard me but before she could look into my eyes she went into shock and started shaking very fast. After a hard shaking her tongue expanded out of her mouth. I grew worried and started to cry and that's when I heard the ambulance arrive. The blue-suited emergency team rushed straight into the house. Big Mama began to pull me away but I refused until I noticed that I had to let the professionals do their job.

The emergency team then began to ask Big Mama questions about grandmother's medical history and allergies.

"Is she allergic to any medication that we should be aware of?" One of the emergency team workers asked.

"Yes, she is allergic to 64 different medications and here is the complete list," Big Mama responded.

Big Mama then handed the list to the emergency team and they all gazed in amazement as if this was impossible.

At this time grandmother was already placed upon the gurney and put into the ambulance. I wanted to go with her so she wouldn't feel alone.

"Big Mama, are we going to the hospital?" I asked.

"No—your Uncle James and Auntie Margie is going to go," Big Mama replied.

"Wait why can't I go? That's not fair. I want to be there for Mama. It's not right!" I shouted.

"Go get some sleep baby, your dad will be here to get you in the morning. I told him what happened here and he thinks you should be at home," Big Mama said.

I quickly turned around and went back into the room. I packed up all of my belongings and just lay in the bed not really wanting to sleep. I was so worried about grandmother and hoped she would be okay.

The next morning I awoke after not getting much sleep.

"Joe Joe your dad is here," Big Mama replied.

I quickly ran to the living room trying to see if Grandmother was back.

"She's not here yet and no one has called but I promise you I will let you know as soon as I find out," Big Mama said.

I kindly thanked her and then apologized to her about yelling at her last night. After hugging her and kissing her on the cheek I continued to walk to the large black truck.

I slowly got into the truck, closed the door and waved goodbye to Big Mama.

There was a long moment of silence as my father continued to drive back home. He looked at me several times but I looked away. I didn't want to hear his mouth. Father sometimes openly criticized grandmother because he knew that was a way to get under my skin.

"So your granny flipped out huh," father said.

"She didn't flip out. She had a seizure, you would know that if you went to school," I said.

"What did you say?" father quickly responded.

I stayed quiet to avoid any further argument.

"Oh, so you're smart huh? You just know everything, huh? Well, guess what, you won't be seeing your granny for a while. In addition, you gonna learn to call me dad. The two of you will respect me and anything I say. So you may as well get use to it," father evilly commented.

I didn't respond because I would not let his words take me down. I refused to cry. I refused to show any weakness at all.

What my father doesn't know is that just because I didn't feed into his conflict I was not scared. My silence wasn't of fear. My silence symbolized belief. Belief that my father would regret those words and would rely on me for help one day. So I sat there patiently and silently and ate those words because those words fed not just my soul but my will to succeed.

# 8
## Life with an Unknown Father

It has now been a couple of months since grandmother's bizarre seizure. I was still under the care of father and would be heading to the 6th grade in less than a month. I was so excited because this summer seemed to be filled with conflict between father and me. In my mind school was the only way out. It seemed as if every little thing I did sparked his anger which resulted in more chores around the house. I finally noticed that these chores were a way to teach me to respect him and abide by his rules.

Rejection is what it was in my eyes.

"Rejection" is defined as refusing to hear, receive, or admit. Now if you want to be more specific you can say emotionally rejected but for the basis of this book we'll just go with rejection. However, I do not want this story just to indicate the bad aspects of what took place in this unknown home but also the good. Although, there was a sense of rejection that I was experiencing father still made sure that our family was spiritually inclined. Each Sunday we would wake up and head to church and even regularly attend bible study throughout the week.

I opened my eyes on the bright Sunday morning

as the sun rays lit up the entire room in which my sister, my younger brother, and I shared. Each day I awoke I made it a priority to write a journal based on what happened the previous day.

The reason I wrote about each day in a previous aspect was because I did not want these journals to be written based off anger. Sometimes anger has its way of controlling a person so I personally thought it was a better idea to write on a clear mind.

So as I sat there in my bed documenting what had happened the previous day I began to hear my stepmother's voice calling my name, alerting that it was time for breakfast.

My stepmother's name was Wanda. She was very nice to me and was the mother of my younger brother Amir. In fact, she was the little bit of comfort that I had while under father's care. She cared for me and my sister dearly. Whenever we needed something she made sure that we had it and didn't rely on father to get it. This may be hurtful to say but I believe that Wanda cared about me and my sister's well-being more than father did.

As I got of bed responding to Wanda's voice I walked to the bathroom to first freshen up. Soon as I got within inches of the door it swung open and father came out.

"Good morning man. You alright?" father said.

I was so confused by him saying good morning that I just froze there in that instant and thought about what was just said. After daydreaming for a couple of seconds I continued into the bathroom grabbed my toothbrush and began to brush my teeth. Once done I walked into the kitchen to see the whole family sitting in their seats getting prepared to eat. I was used to eating together as a family but not with this much energy. Well of course Wanda always had a gleeful spirit as she prepared breakfast but seeing father with the same spirit was very rare.

I walked around the table and took a seat nearest the window because I was always the last one to finish eating. My little brother and I sometimes talked about sports during breakfast while my older sister and brother seemed uninterested about the morning conversation and was always eager to depart from the table.

My older brother name was D'Jon. He was the outspoken child that resided in the home. He was the one to say whatever was on his mind during any situations. In my opinion I think he felt like the total outcast in the family. D'Jon had a different mother from the rest of us. To this day I don't know too much about her but a friend of the family once told me that his mother allowed father to raise him because she feared he was getting out of hand. I always asked myself why she put him in the hands of father.

There were so many things that I did not understand about D'jon and father's relationship. It was built on a love-hate basis but the hate overpowered the love most of the time. They were constantly bumping heads sometimes even getting physical. But one quality that I noticed that D'Jon and I shared was the will not to give in and quit. He also never showed his true emotions and never shed tears in front of father. I don't know why he vowed to never cry in front of father but I personally could not stand to see him (father) in satisfaction of his dysfunction.

As I took my seat at the end of the table I just sat there in silence. I don't know why but I just didn't feel completely part of the family.

After a couple of minutes of complete silence and watching Wanda make the plates, father entered in to the kitchen. I was hoping to finally see him be affectionate not to us his own children but to Wanda as she once again made breakfast for the entire family, but was quickly disappointed when father skipped right past Amir and sat in the tall wooden brown dining chair.

"So, good morning everyone, how did you guys sleep and are you guys ready to go to church," father said.

No one said anything for quite a few seconds. After we all looked around the round the table wondering who would reply to the question Starnisha broke the ice.

"Yeah, we are daddy, and I slept well." Starnisha replied.

As I sat their listening to them have a full conversation I tried to wonder why I couldn't have a full conversation with him. Was it because I couldn't forgive him for the way that he had treated me in the past years?

I never have gotten the answer to that question. I always thought that forgiving someone was just saying the words "I forgive you" but that's not the case.

As my father and Starnisha continued to have a conversation my brothers and I sat their looking at each other.

"Here's your food baby," Wanda said.

She handed father and Amir their plates followed

by the rest of us. After everyone had their plates we all sat waiting for who be the one to say grace; blessing the over the food.

"Why don't Joe Joe go ahead and bless the food," father said.

I quickly looked at father to catch a glimpse of his facial expression.

Honestly, I wanted to say grace so the prideful look on father's face after giving me the duty to pray was irrelevant. However, I played by father's rules and continued on with my prayer.

"No problem. Bow your head and close your eyes please. God I ask that you bless this food that we are about to receive. I ask that you continue to not just bless us in this home but the world so that we may be focused on the path that you have set out for us. Lord I also ask that you bless my grandmother and the rest of my family. In the name of Jesus Amen," I said.

I knew that I giving grandmother her own individual praise might upset father but deep inside I meant every word of that prayer.

Everyone heads popped up followed by the word, Amen.

As everyone began to eat their breakfast it got real quiet. When it got like this Wanda would always break the ice because she loved to see father interact with us.

Now I must say one thing that I always admired about Wanda was that she always made father interact with us. She believes that the child-father bond was a vital component in the development of the child. Notice I said child-father instead of father-child bond. This is so because although Wanda always pushed father into performing his fatherly roles, we his children still had to take the first step. If we wanted to spend time with father it never came naturally. We would have to ask him to spend time with us.

"So you guys ready for this great service we are about to receive," Wanda said.

We all shook our head and replied yeah.

After the breakfast we all began to get dressed for the early morning service. I felt awkward going to this church sometimes due to the fact that I always attended Holy Chapel with my grandmother.

As me and my older brother D'Jon continued to get dressed we talked about father and the gleeful spirit that he had at breakfast.

"I'm not buying it for one second and you shouldn't either. Your dad is good at getting people's hopes up then shattering them," I said.

This is what happens when someone constantly tells you they are going to do something and never do it. Although, some might not ever say it, it's a real disappointing feeling.

"Let's go, time to head out," father said.

Me and my brother then looked at each other and continued out the door.

# 9
## Issues, Lessons, & Family Problems

Weeks began to pass by and school was right around the corner. I was so excited because I knew I would then be away from father. Over these weeks not only did father's attitude become more complex but I noticed him starting to consume lots of alcohol. Once intoxicated he became more furious and believed that what he said goes. This caused problems for my big brother D'Jon and father because their personalities started to clash. But it wasn't until one big physical conformation that I knew that their relationship would never be the same.

I awoke late one night to loud screams and sounds of fumbling objects. As I got out of bed I looked around to see if my younger brother had been awaken by the commotion but was shocked to see him still sleep.

I then began to move closer to the door to try to hear more of what was going on. As I listened carefully I began to hear father yell.

I didn't know who he was yelling at but I knew in a matter of seconds I was going to find out.

"Where in the hell were you?" father said.

"I was at a friend's house we were just hanging out," D'Jon said.

Whenever father wasn't sure about something that one of us said he would give us this stare that symbolized disbelief along with a silent streak. I knew things were only going to get worse so I creaked the door open so I can see exactly what was going on.

As I peered through the creek of the door I noticed that father and D'Jon were not the only ones who were in the living room. Wanda and Starnisha sat there curiously listening and by the looks on their face I can tell neither knew exactly what was going on.

"Now look man, I'm not gonna play this game with you like you're a little ass kid. You either gonna tell me where you been or I'm going to whup yo ass," father said.

After those words I thought maybe I was dreaming and this all couldn't be happening. Then I noticed that there was another complete silence and then Wanda began to speak.

Wanda always had to be the mediator. She sorted situations out through communication unlike father's violence.

"Okay this is getting way out of hand Joseph. D'Jon called me and let me know where he was going to be so this whole little confrontation should be done with. I forgot to tell you but I knew where he was," Wanda said.

Father then stared at Wanda for a couple of seconds and this is when I got the first look at his face. His eyes were red and laid low which lead me to the assumption that he was intoxicated. So I then started to connect the dots and concluded that this behavior was no different from the other behaviors he displayed in the past.

"So Wanda you gonna tell me how to raise my kids," father said.

Even I knew that statement had no relevance to what was being discussed but in father's head he was always right.

"I'm not trying to tell you anything but what I am saying is that you're overreacting to nothing and you look drunk," Wanda replied.

So another moment of silence took place and everyone sat there looking at father but father had directed his attention back to D'Jon.

"So where did you get your hair cut from?" father asked.

I think by that time everyone in the living room was thinking the same thought which was what does that have to do with what was being discussed at this time.

In addition, I can tell Wanda was now pissed off by father not answering her because she went into the bedroom and slammed the door.

I can tell by the look in D'Jon's eyes that he was frightened by the question or more so what was to come next.

"My cousin Anthony cut my hair," D'Jon stuttered.

Father then gave D'Jon a very peculiar look as if he still wasn't buying his story.

"You know what? Grab the mop and start cleaning up this damn house because you think you slick," father said.

At this point I was so confused. I had no clue what was going on, nor the purpose of father's argument. In my eyes it was just another method that he was using to show that he was in charge.

As D'Jon grabbed the mop and cleaning supplies he began to mutter under his breath.

I knew that this would cause further problems.

As I sat near the door still peering through the crack I noticed the scared look on Starnisha's face. I think at this point she had begun to sense the same thing I was as D'Jon steadily muttered on.

"What did you say boy?" father asked.

I knew this time father would go all the way. I cautiously arose to my feet after sitting on the floor eavesdropping for so long.

A quick idea came to mind as I stood there still peering through the door watching father get closer and closer to D'Jon. I figured if I came out of the room and went into the living room it would sort of pull some of the attention off D'Jon and onto me so that father would forget about D'Jon.

I wasn't sure it was going to work but I was willing to try so that things wouldn't get to out of hand.

I quickly opened the door and headed straight into the living room. A weird awkward silence took over the room but I continued straight to the couch and sat next to Starnisha.

"Oh what's wrong with you? Did I wake you up?" father asked.

I just stared at him noticing my plan was working. The attention was on me and I knew exactly how to handle it.

"I just felt like getting up. I wasn't tired," I replied.

At this point in my life I had lost all respect for father. I didn't know if I hated him. I didn't know if I loved him.

Shockingly, father turned his head and continued to towards D'Jon.

"Now, what were you muttering under your breath?" father asked.

I looked at D'Jon hoping he would just close his mouth and not respond. I knew that father was waiting for the littlest gesture from D'Jon stating that he was being disrespected so that he would have reason to flip out.

As much as I wanted D'Jon to keep his mouth closed I knew that he would say something. It just wasn't like him to back down from father.

"All I said is that I'm getting in trouble for no reason. It's not like I snuck out of the house and didn't tell anyone. You're always overacting about everything. I just want to go back home to my mom. I never wanted to live with you!" D'Jon shouted.

Father stared into D'jon's face as silence filled the room. Starnisha and I sat closely on the couch hoping that father would respond in a way that could settle the problems between the two but I had a feeling that wouldn't happen.

Father then turned his back to D'Jon and looked at me and Starnisha.

Could this be the trick to getting under father's skin? Well in a few seconds I was sure I was going to find out.

Father stood there for several moments with a blank expression on his face.

Suddenly, he lifted his hand out of his pockets

and smacked D'Jon across the face causing him to slam into the refrigerator and then hit the floor. It happened so fast none of us knew it was coming especially D'Jon. Starnisha and I gasped as we looked at our brother stumbling to get back to his feet.

Quickly Wanda came out of the room and ran towards the kitchen to see D'Jon there on the floor.

"What are you doing Joseph? You have gone too far this time. I promise you if you ever put your hand on these kids again I'm going to put my hands on you," Wanda said.

I knew Wanda was serious as she helped D'Jon up onto his feet. Father just stared as if he had done nothing wrong.

Suddenly he looked at D'Jon once again as if he weren't finished with him.

"Oh, so you gonna cry now boy?" father said.

"Baby I want you to go pack all your stuff. I'm taking you home to your mom where you belong," Wanda said.

D'Jon quickly went into the bedroom and closed the door.

"Now look Joseph, something is wrong with you. You need some kind of help. You treat your kids horrible. I'm not going to put up with none of your stuff. I'm not your mama and pretty soon I won't be your wife either," Wanda said.

Wanda then turned around and went into the room to help D'Jon gather his things. Father said not a word and maintained the same innocent facial expression on face. He then quickly grabbed his coat off the couch where me and Starnisha were sitting and headed toward the door. Just as he was about to walk out he turned his head and looked at my sister and I and then slammed the door shut.

At this time I tried to analyze all the events that had happened in that short amount of time. I was lost as to what started the confrontation. However, I knew that father could have finished it without resulting to violence. This is where the statement, "violence never solves anything" became clear to me. Although father did strike D'Jon and used intimidating techniques to break him, D'Jon held his ground and showed no weakness therefore defeating father's purpose.

Deep down inside this sparked another level of hate for my father within my heart. As I sat there thinking, I began to fill a sense of betrayal. I began to feel as if I were left alone in a world to fend on my own. I began to question why my mother left the world before guiding me into life. However, I never received an answer but remembered grandmother's words, "You are not alone—you were not built to give up. Never lose sight of your dreams and know you can overcome anything."

# 10
## First Day

Father continued to consume alcohol and only became more detached then he had already had been. He then acquired the habit of staying out on most nights which forced us to be more independent when Wanda wasn't at home.

Pain and abandonment is what father was inflicting upon our family. "Pain" is defined as an acute mental or emotional distress or suffering and abandonment is defined as given up or forsaken.

In addition, we lost communication with D'Jon for some time after the incident occurred. He sometimes called us to make sure we were okay and that nothing had happened to us. He was very disappointed when he learned that Starnisha had got struck the same way he had when she muttered something about washing the dishes. In a way, I couldn't help but think that maybe I should have volunteered to be struck so that maybe my family would have pulled me from the custody of father as D'Jon's mother had pulled him.

But once I thought about the pain he must of have felt that idea fled my mind instantly.

So the time had finally come for me to start

school. I was so excited to be in a new learning environment and more so anxious to make new friends. I was also eager to see if I could keep up the same level of academic proficiency as I had while in elementary school. I knew it wouldn't be hard for me. I would just have to stay focused and keep finding that motivation within myself to succeed.

However, I did notice that being on a new campus meant that once again I was a nobody and would have to work my way back up to the top to gain the respect from all my peers.

Notice that when I use the word "nobody" I don't mean a person who knows no one but a person who is unknown to everyone. I guess you can say I was used to everyone knowing who I was. At this moment in my life I was no longer "Joe" but "Joe Rivers."

Although, some people may have called me a nerd in elementary school, for the most part I was pretty popular, but here at Hamilton Middle school I was just another student. No one would know me for my academic excellence and that is what most frightened me. I felt in a way that I was starting all over again but it was just something I was going to have to deal with.

In addition, I had been talking to grandmother a lot more and was happy to know that she was well. Her and grandfather had also moved to Obispo Street where Aunt Freda and Aunt Thea were residing. I thought it was nice that the family moved near each other once again. However, I know that my family had a history of drama so I wondered if it would follow.

Now that grandmother was well she demanded that father bring me over to her place regularly and so he did. So for the last week before school I had spent a lot of time with grandmother. I was so happy that I had someone I could talk to again about anything.

As I hopped out of bed I rushed toward the bathroom anxious for the first day of school. I couldn't help but think this would be a great first day. After showering I put on the black and red school uniform that I had ironed the night before and continued into the kitchen to have breakfast. I couldn't wait to see my friends from my elementary school.

As I got into the kitchen only father was there. I cautiously walked over to the table and sat down waiting to see if Wanda would enter the kitchen and began to cook. There was a long moment of silence as each of said nothing to one another.

I then decided to break the silence because it began to feel uncomfortable.

"Do you know where Wanda is," I softly asked.

Father just continued doing what he was doing for a second but answered after I turned my head and peered out of the window paying him no attention.

"Yeah, she went to take Amir and Starnisha to school and I'm going to take you. If you want something to eat there's some cereal on top of the refrigerator and milk inside," father said.

Now this statement flared my anger. As long as I had been staying with father he had known that I was allergic to milk and that I didn't eat cereal. But yet he insisted that I eat it.

"I'm allergic to milk and I don't eat cereal. I'll just eat at school. It's cool." I replied.

Father then gave me this look as if I had done something wrong by telling him that I didn't eat cereal. So I stared at him to see what he would say next.

"I ain't ever heard that and I don't believe that you're allergic to milk so you gonna eat some cereal today," father angrily replied.

I then turned my head and continued to look out of the window. I wanted to get up from that table and tell him he didn't know anything about me because he was never there. Then slap him across the face to show him how it feels.

I was so sick of this "man." The only reason I found myself putting up with him was because of the 5th commandment from the list of 10 that grandmother had taught me when I was younger. This commandment clearly stated "Honor your father and your mother, that your days may be long upon the land which the Lord your God is giving you." I knew exactly what this meant and I honored it.

As I sat there still daydreaming father began to walk over to the table where I was sitting and before I knew it shoved the bowl of cereal in front of me. He didn't say a word as he walked back over to the counter and grabbed a banana off the top of the microwave. I then began to grow very curious as I watched him closely. He slowly began to peel the sleeve off of the banana. After removing the sleeve he walked toward the drawer where the silverware was located. He reach in and out grabbed out a sharp knife and placed the banana on the counter. Father then began to cut the banana in pieces.

My curiosity grew more and more each second.

A second later father began to walk my way. I tried looking away but he still moved closer and closer without saying a word. Then without a notice or approval—dumped the banana pieces into my bowl of cereal.

"There you go, eat yo food," father said.

I didn't want to cause any conflict so I began to eat the cereal. With each bite I began to feel sicker and sicker. So I then came up with a plan to get rid of the cereal but it would require that father somehow get distracted. But I had no clue how that would be possible. Seconds later the phone began to ring and I knew the phone was in father's room so this was my shot. After the second ring father took off heading towards the bedroom. I quickly got up from my seat and headed toward the garbage disposal. The reason I didn't use the trash can is because I would always get caught. It became a method for checking to see if we ate the meals he prepared so I knew this cereal had to go down the garbage disposal. However, I knew I was taking a chance because of the loud sound it makes when it consumes the food. So as I got to the sink, I could hear father concluding the conversation he was having on the phone. I quickly turned the water on in an attempt to cut down the noise from the disposal and quickly poured the cereal down leaving just a little bit. I had to leave something in the bowl so father would believe I ate it rather than dumped it. I then began to hear father's footsteps coming nearer and nearer as I sprinted back to my seat after first turning off the disposal and twisting the water knob off. Father then entered the kitchen.

"You eating your food man," father said.

"Yes, I am," I replied.

I then cautiously looked up at the sink to see the water still partially running. I began to ask myself how

I could be so dumb. I knew I was going to get caught at this moment.

"Man, I left out of here so quick I left the water on," father said to himself.

I knew it had to be an angel protecting me at this point. By this time I had eaten the remainder of the cereal. I cautiously got up from the table and put my bowl in the sink happy to have gotten away without getting in trouble.

"Let's go Joe Joe, time to take you to school," father said.

My joy began to come back because of how anxious I was about my first day of school.

The ride to school was silent like I said before we shared no father-son bond and rarely spoke unless we had to. The sound of soft jazz music was the only common interest I think we shared as we both nodded our heads to the mellow sounds whenever in the car together.

As we arrived to my school I began to unbuckle my seatbelt after seeing some friends from elementary school. The truck came to a halt and right as I was about to get out the truck father place his arm on my left leg which caught my attention.

"Have a good day son," father said.

This once again was one of those moments in which I did not know how to react or how to respond. I was not used to calling him "Dad" and I was not used to him calling me "Son" so I sat there in complete awe trying to figure out what to say back to him.

"Thanks," I replied.

That was the only thing I could come up with and it's sad to say but I had no clue on what type of relationship we had. Sometimes I could tell father tried but that's my point, a father should not try "sometimes." It's like having a job and taking off when you feel like it. It just doesn't work that way. When you accept the role of being a father you're obligated to that child for better or worse.

Telling you about my first day of school in full detail would be irrelevant to the story but I would say that I met a lot of new friends and fitted in just fine. I answered most of the questions that my teachers threw at me which gave the other students in my classes the assumption that I was extremely smart which is what I liked to be known for. But I am leaving out the bad part of my first day. Although, so many wonderful things did happen that day, one very bad incident happened. Due to the cereal I was forced to eat that morning, I threw up in one of my classes which also gave the students the impression that I was weird. So which one has more weight? It would be being considered weird because I knew students would forever remember me for that incident. This is where I was introduced to the word "peer pressure."

# 11
## Peer Pressure

The school year began to take off and once again I found myself the class nerd. Only this time being so smart wasn't as welcoming as it was when I was in elementary school. Here in middle school it seemed as if being an individual with intellect was a disease. On some days I even found myself trying to pretend I was dumb so that I would not be the odd one in my classes. In my mind this was a way for me to fit in with my peers.

"Individuality" is defined as a specific personality, character, or characteristic that distinguishes one person or thing from another. This will be the section of the book where you gain the confidence to be yourself and create your own plan. Many individuals today want to be like the rappers on television, the cool kids at school, etc. Doesn't it sound better to be proud of who *you* are? There was a saying I came up with when I was in the 4th grade and it goes "Why reach over and grab someone else's rope when you have one right in front of yourself."

Aside from school I began to feel a lot better about being home with father because the time that I spent with grandmother gradually increased, going from a couple of hours to several days. It felt so good to have someone supporting me educationally once again because it inspired me to work harder. However, I knew that grandmother would be highly upset if she found out that I was pretending to be dumb just to fit in with the cool students in my classes.

I knew that if grandmother found out that I was pretending to be dumb in an attempt to fit in with the other students she would ask a question to make me analyze my actions. She probably would say something like, "Now do you feel cool now that you're dumb?" But acceptance is defined as willingness to treat someone as a member of a group or social circle which is what I longed for in this new environment of peers.

Going to my classes was a mystery each day. I never knew what to expect or how I would need to portray myself in order to stay cool in the eyes of my peers. I didn't realize how much I had changed during my sixth grade year until I put myself in the position of a girl that I had teased and talked about for being disabled. This was not something that I was proud of but due to the accepting responses from the kids I thought were my friends I continued to insult this poor girl until she was in tears. After the incident I felt horrible, so I spent the entire day looking for her to give her a formal apology and insure her that if she needed anything I was there for her.

"Peer pressure" is defined as the social pressure on somebody to adopt a type of behavior, dress, or attitude in order to be accepted as part of a group.

After apologizing to the girl I felt a lot better but knew that I would have to make a choice either to want to fit in with the crowd around me or become my own individual.

I must have not been ready to become my own individual because the next day I found myself trying to fit in with another crowd. This was no ordinary crowd though. This crowd was lead by an 8th grader. His name was Tucker Washington.

Everyone who went to my middle school knew Tucker because what he said goes or there would be a fight. He was disrespectful not only to his peers but to teachers and administrators as well. In addition, I had been waiting for father in front of my school one day and saw him and his mother in a loud and heated argument. So this bought me to the conclusion that Tucker was an animal who could not be controlled.

However, because of where and how I was raised you never bow down to anyone. You never run from a fight. If someone hits, you hit them back and always look a man in his eyes to show you are not intimidated. These are some of the basic morals you acquire when growing up in the neighborhood I did even if you're not a violent person.

With that being said, Tucker and I never spoke to each other—we just always made eye contact and then continued with our business. In addition, I think I was off his get-list because my older cousin Ronnie went to the same middle school and continued to keep an eye on me. Kind of like a guardian angel—wherever I went I could tell he was always watching. The best thing about Ronnie is that he was huge, 6 feet, two inches and near 300 pounds. So his image was intimidating alone.

I knew one day Tucker and I would finally come

face to face but I didn't know when. So one day as I walking to my 4th period class Tucker called my name.

"Yeah what's up," I shockingly replied.

"You should hang with me and crew today, my boys tell me you pretty cool." Tucker said.

"Yeah, that's cool I'm down," I responded.

Every time something bad was going to happen I always got a bad vibe sort of like the vision I had the day of Uncle Gene's trial. I knew that hanging with Tucker would only be a negative influence on my life.

As I sat in 4th period I continued to watch the clock because lunch was next. I was sort of nervous but curious to see what Tucker meant by hang with him and his crew.

The bell rang and I quietly arose from my seat and headed towards the door after turning in my assignment.

I continued down the hall in the direction I had seen Tucker and his friends waiting for me. As I got closer I began to ask myself, "What am I doing hanging with these guys?" I then started to think about the friends I hung out with on a normal basis and I began to compare them.

"So what's up bro, you ready to go on some missions," Tucker asked.

I stood there in a daze wondering what he could have meant by "missions." Were we going to harm someone, steal, or vandalize? I had no clue at this point but I did not want to be involved.

"We got some smoke for you too," Tucker said.

I looked around to see all of the guys leaned against the wall smoking the green crumbled substance.

"No I don't smoke," I replied.

"Cool, more for us," Tucker said.

As we continued to walk around the campus I started to feel a sense of displacement as I thought about the reasons I wanted to fit in with this group. I knew deep down inside that I did not belong in this group. They were the complete opposite of me, had no dream, no motivation, no confident in themselves to succeed.

Suddenly I stopped walking and the entire crew looked back at me to see what was going on.

"You alright J," Tucker said.

I heard the voice in my head tell me to break all connections with this group and create my own path. Because if not I was banging on the roots of trouble. I then began to think of my dreams, goals and aspirations and asked myself one simple question. Are you willing to put it all at risk to be popular?

I then stepped right up to Tucker so he could hear every word I was about to say. At this moment a crowd began to gather—and many probably looked on—as if it was a confrontation and there was going to be a fight. I could see my cousin Ronnie and his friends rushing nearer after seeing me but I didn't care.

"Look here Tuck, no offense but I'm not down with anything you do. I don't do drugs, I don't drink, I don't talk about people in a bad manner, I'm not disrespectful, I'm a straight A student and most of all I'm an individual, meaning I'm not like you. I'm my own person. So go find another puppet to fit the rest of these you have here," I said.

There was a loud "OHHHH" from the crowds that had gathered. I slowly looked around to see there were a great number of people actually watching, just waiting for something to happen. This is how it normally happens at schools—people begin to instigate because they want to see action.

Suddenly I focused my attention back to Tucker who stood their looking at me. He was about 3 feet taller than me so it required me to look up to him just to make complete eye contact.

Seconds later Ronnie and his friends busted through the crowds and were there on the right side of me. However, I kept my eyes focused on Tucker just to show him I was not intimidated in any way. I always hated to resort to violence but that didn't mean I didn't know how to.

Tucker than took a step back and began to speak.

"You know I'm not mad at you. I don't like what I do or the way I am. It's just what I was taught. My whole family does drugs, and the ones who don't are in jail. This is me, but this ain't you. You're better than all of us here. Even in elementary school I knew you were going to do good things. Don't let anyone step in the way of you doing things. You always been one of the ones I admired. So I agree with you bro, I wouldn't hang with me either because I have nothing to live for," Tucker replied.

He then turned around and walked away.

"What's this about man," Ronnie said.

"It's good. Just understanding one another," I replied.

I can tell that the crowd was disappointed that Tucker and I didn't fight but it wasn't about that. That moment gave me a chance to understand that all kids that have corrupt characteristics aren't horrible people who dread the world, doing evil things. But showed me that these corrupt characteristics are sometimes what we adapt to after being implied for so long.

Peer pressure is not a joke. If you truly don't want to do something, don't do it to fit in with a crowd of people who cares nothing about your well-being or safety.

I was upset to learn that two weeks later Tucker Washington was shot six times and killed after being told to pull out a gun on a group of men who took it as a gang-related threat. This chapter is dedicated to you because through your words I learned to be an individual. You taught me the lesson of being mindful of the people I hang with, as well as the choices I make, and for that I am forever grateful.

## 12
## The End of the Beginning

My 6th grade year was the year I learned to embrace myself as not being weird for making my own path but wise. I have composed all my journals to create this book in an effort to show just how valuable education is. My journey has not been easy thus far. Obstacles arise each day bringing knowledge to my awareness. This book was not built on the platter of revenge or exposure. This book simply describes the events that took place in my life and how they shaped me into the determined confident man I am today.

For those of you who have made it to the end of this book notice that the plan is not just a formula that you can acquire in a sentence but rather a process. A theory I used to describe this process would be the example of climbing to the top of an object.

Life is all one big climb, there are times that will be tough and there are times that will be gracious. However, it is you who has to make that climb not anyone else. Not your family, your friends, etc. But once you make it to the top, you turn around and look how far you have come and those are the results that will fill your heart with joy.

My grandmother is the reason I continue to climb to this day. I have to show her that I would make it no matter what is thrown my way. My childhood was not perfect but I am certainly not ashamed of it. I am proud to have gone through all the trials I did because without them I would not know the importance of striving to follow your dreams.

To my loving father although we had our share of differences, I hold no grudges and love you with all thine heart. For I know that to make it, you must be able to forgive.

For those of you who hoped for a happy ending I'm sorry to disappoint you but this story is just opening the door to a world of knowledge.

This is the only the end of the beginning.

I am a young man with a plan.

To be continued.

## About the Author

Born in a suburb of Los Angeles in October 1990 Joseph Anthony Rivers endured multiple years of grief, parental abuse, and issues of low self-worth. However, through education, hard work, and perseverance in fulfilling his dreams, he somehow rose above it all to write this bold account of his life and times.

## About the Editor

Gary Brin was born in 1965 and has lived in the United States Virgin Islands, Hawaii, and California. He has edited books on such notable historical figures as Nancy Hanks Lincoln, Betsy Ross, Daniel Boone, Nathan Hale, Dolly Madison, David Douglas, Abraham Lincoln, George Washington, Wilbur & Orville Wright, Henry Obookiah, Archibald Menzies, Sacajawea, and the Lewis & Clark Expedition journals.

LaVergne, TN USA
23 November 2010
206122LV00001B/49/P